# HOLIDAY FAVORITES

**_Solos and Band Arrangements_**
**_Correlated with Essential Elements® Band Method_**

**_Arranged by ROBERT LONGFIELD, JOHNNIE VINSON, MICHAEL SWEENEY and PAUL LAVENDER_**

Welcome to Essential Elements Holiday Favorites! There are two versions of each selection in this versatile book. The SOLO version appears in the beginning of each student book. The FULL BAND arrangement of each song follows. The ONLINE RECORDINGS or PIANO ACCOMPANIMENT BOOK may be used as an accompaniment for solo performance. Use these recordings when playing solos for friends and family.



**PLAYBACK+**
*Speed • Pitch • Balance • Loop*

To access audio visit:
**www.halleonard.com/mylibrary**

Enter Code
6796-5601-7380-6228

ISBN 978-1-5400-2788-7

HAL•LEONARD®



00870006

Visit Hal Leonard Online at
**www.halleonard.com**

Contact Us:
**Hal Leonard**
7777 West Bluemound Road
Milwaukee, WI 53213
Email: info@halleonard.com

In Europe contact:
**Hal Leonard Europe Limited**
42 Wigmore Street
Marylebone, London, W1U 2RN
Email: info@halleonardeurope.com

In Australia contact:
**Hal Leonard Australia Pty. Ltd.**
4 Lentara Court
Cheltenham, Victoria, 3192 Australia
Email: info@halleonard.com.au

# AULD LANG SYNE

BASSOON
Solo

Words by ROBERT BURNS
Traditional Scottish Melody
Arranged by MICHAEL SWEENEY

00870006

# FELIZ NAVIDAD

**BASSOON**
**Solo**

**Music and Lyrics by**
**JOSÉ FELICIANO**
Arranged by PAUL LAVENDER

# PARADE OF THE WOODEN SOLDIERS

BASSOON
Solo

English Lyrics by BALLARD MacDONALD
Music by LEON JESSEL
Arranged by PAUL LAVENDER

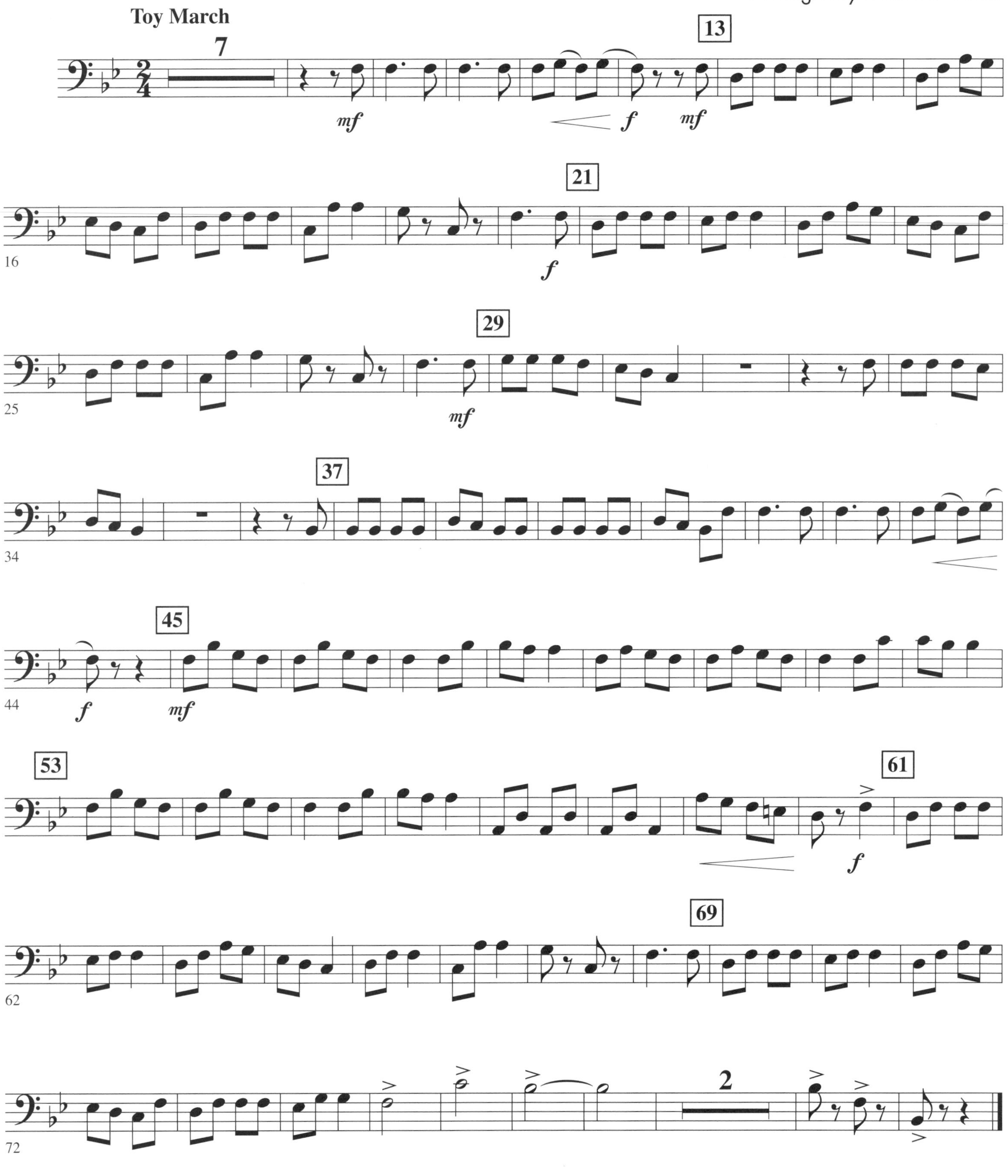

# GOOD KING WENCESLAS

BASSOON
Solo

Words by JOHN M. NEALE
Music from PIAE CANTIONES
Arranged by ROBERT LONGFIELD

00870006

# PAT-A-PAN
## (Willie, Take Your Little Drum)

BASSOON
Solo

Words and Music by
**BERNARD de la MONNOYE**
Arranged by ROBERT LONGFIELD

# SILVER BELLS

BASSOON
Solo

**Words and Music by**
**JAY LIVINGSTON and RAY EVANS**
Arranged by PAUL LAVENDER

00870006

# DO YOU HEAR WHAT I HEAR

BASSOON
Solo

Words and Music by
NOEL REGNEY and GLORIA SHAYNE
Arranged by MICHAEL SWEENEY

From THE SOUND OF MUSIC

# MY FAVORITE THINGS

BASSOON
Solo

**Lyrics by OSCAR HAMMERSTEIN II**
**Music by RICHARD RODGERS**
Arranged by ROBERT LONGFIELD

00870006

From the Motion Picture Irving Berlin's HOLIDAY INN

# WHITE CHRISTMAS

BASSOON
Solo

Words and Music by
IRVING BERLIN
Arranged by JOHNNIE VINSON

00870006

# CHRISTMAS TIME IS HERE

BASSOON
Solo

Words by LEE MENDELSON
Music by VINCE GUARALDI
Arranged by JOHNNIE VINSON

00870006

From Warner Bros. Pictures' THE POLAR EXPRESS

# THE POLAR EXPRESS

BASSOON
Solo

Words and Music by
GLEN BALLARD and ALAN SILVESTRI
Arranged by JOHNNIE VINSON

00870006

# AULD LANG SYNE

BASSOON
Band Arrangement

Words by ROBERT BURNS
Traditional Scottish Melody
Arranged by MICHAEL SWEENEY

00870006

# FELIZ NAVIDAD

BASSOON
Band Arrangement

Music and Lyrics by
**JOSÉ FELICIANO**
Arranged by PAUL LAVENDER

00870006

# PARADE OF THE WOODEN SOLDIERS

BASSOON
Band Arrangement

English Lyrics by BALLARD MacDONALD
Music by LEON JESSEL
Arranged by PAUL LAVENDER

00870006

# GOOD KING WENCESLAS

BASSOON
Band Arrangement

Words by JOHN M. NEALE
Music from PIAE CANTIONES
Arranged by ROBERT LONGFIELD

# PAT-A-PAN
## (Willie, Take Your Little Drum)

BASSOON
Band Arrangement

Words and Music by
**BERNARD de la MONNOYE**
Arranged by ROBERT LONGFIELD

# SILVER BELLS

BASSOON
Band Arrangement

Words and Music by
JAY LIVINGSTON and RAY EVANS
Arranged by PAUL LAVENDER

00870006

# DO YOU HEAR WHAT I HEAR

BASSOON
Band Arrangement

Words and Music by
NOEL REGNEY and GLORIA SHAYNE
Arranged by MICHAEL SWEENEY

00870006

From THE SOUND OF MUSIC

# MY FAVORITE THINGS

BASSOON
Band Arrangement

Lyrics by OSCAR HAMMERSTEIN II
Music by RICHARD RODGERS
Arranged by ROBERT LONGFIELD

00870006

From the Motion Picture Irving Berlin's HOLIDAY INN

# WHITE CHRISTMAS

**BASSOON**
**Band Arrangement**

Words and Music by
**IRVING BERLIN**
Arranged by JOHNNIE VINSON

00870006

# CHRISTMAS TIME IS HERE

BASSOON
Band Arrangement

**Words by LEE MENDELSON**
**Music by VINCE GUARALDI**
Arranged by JOHNNIE VINSON

From Warner Bros. Pictures' THE POLAR EXPRESS

# THE POLAR EXPRESS

BASSOON
Band Arrangement

Words and Music by
GLEN BALLARD and ALAN SILVESTRI
Arranged by JOHNNIE VINSON

00870006